PLAN ₿ PLAYBOOK

PLAN ₿ PLAYBOOK

BEST INTRO BOOK TO BITCOIN & TRADING

HAISAM SAID

PLAN ₿ PLAYBOOK

© Copyright 2024 Haisam Said
All Rights Reserved.

PLAN ₿ PLAYBOOK

SATOSHI NAKAMOTO'S WHITE PAPER

BITCOIN
A PEER-TO-PEER
ELECTRONIC
CASH SYSTEM

Abstract. A purely peer-to-peer version of electronic cash would allow online payments to be sent directly from one party to another without going through a financial institution. Digital signatures provide part of the solution, but the main benefits are lost if a trusted third party is still required to prevent double-spending. We propose a solution to the double-spending problem using a peer-to-peer network. The network timestamps transactions by hashing them into an ongoing chain of hash-based proof-of-work, forming a record that cannot be changed without redoing the proof-of-work. The longest chain not only serves as proof of the sequence of events witnessed, but proof that it came from the largest pool of CPU power. As long as a majority of CPU power is controlled by nodes that are not cooperating to attack the network, they'll generate the longest chain and outpace attackers. The network itself requires minimal structure. Messages are broadcast on a best effort basis, and nodes can leave and rejoin the network at will, accepting the longest proof-of-work chain as proof of what happened while they were gone.

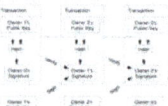

CONTENTS

TERMINOLOGY	1
AUTHOR'S MESSAGE	4
INTRODUCTION	7
ONE	
INTRO TO MONEY	9
TWO	
INTRO TO BITCOIN!	15
THREE	
HOW TO START INVESTING?	33
FOUR	
INTRO TO TRADING	37
FIVE	
RISK MANAGEMENT & LEVERAGE	40
SIX	
CANDLESTICK AND CHART PATTERNS!	42
ENDNOTE	71

PLAN B PLAYBOOK

TERMINOLOGY

PLAN ₿ PLAYBOOK

BTC - Bitcoin

FIAT - US Dollar or Currency

SATS - Satoshis

HODL - Hold on For Dear Life

DCA - Dollar Cost Averaging

BULLS - Buyers

BEARS - Sellers

SHORT - To Place a Sell Trade

LONG - To Place a Buy Trade

HALVING - Bitcoin reduces mining rewards in half every 4 years

ETF - Electronically Traded Fund

BEST TIME TO BUY BITCOIN IS NOW!!!

PLAN ₿ PLAYBOOK

THE ANNONYMOUS CREATOR
OF THE GREATEST ASSET IN HISTORY!

BITCOIN!!!

Satoshi Nakamoto introduced to the world back on oct 31, 2008 a peer-to-peer electronic cash system, that forever continues to change the world and disappeared!

'If you don't believe it or don't get it, I don't have the time to try to convince you."
— **Satoshi Nakamoto**

Author's Message

PLAN ₿ PLAYBOOK

Believe it or not, I got into Bitcoin by accident. I came across it while sports betting on a website that did transactions with Bitcoin. At the time, Bitcoin was trading around $3,000, and I was oblivious to what it was. I was winning my bets, and I remember at one point having a few Bitcoins, but in my head, I was wondering how I could convert this into $$$ because I had no knowledge of what Bitcoin was. To me, it was just a way to transfer my winnings. Fast forward to 2020, I started hearing a lot about it because I started getting into finance and wanted to learn about stocks. As I started to invest in stocks, I started hearing more and more about Bitcoin, and the more I heard, the more eager I was to read up on it. I would spend hours and hours staying up all night reading and studying the coin.

At this point, my mind was made that Bitcoin would be the future and the race was on. On December 18, 2021, I purchased my first full Bitcoin at $48,000!! Can you imagine spending $48,000 on something you can't see, touch, or feel? But it had nothing to do with those things. It was about my belief. I truly believe in Bitcoin and its innovation. My biggest regret was not buying sooner or learning about it earlier. Bitcoin is the greatest asset of our time, and in the past 5 years I have been in the industry, I have seen it all and gone through all the emotions. I never panicked and sold, even when it went down to $15,000. Bitcoin is hope for anyone that wants to invest in their future. Big or small, start!!! Buying Bitcoin right now is like purchasing real estate in Manhattan before the 1900s; we are still early!!!!

Study Bitcoin!!!

Dollar cost averaging "DCA" is the best way to invest; the $100 a month you invest will be worth $1000 a month. In the future, you have to be consistent. But this book isn't financial advice; it's just my experience that I wanted to share with the world because I saw what it did for me firsthand and want to see others succeed as well.

This book was written to help anyone that wants to better themselves and their future. This playbook will introduce you to the world of finance, economics, trading, and the future of money. Bitcoin!

I hope you will find all the information provided to you helpful so you can begin your journey into investing and saving for your future. Times are changing, and if you're not adapting and changing with it, you'll be left behind. Use this book as a guide into your future of managing your finances and bettering your lifestyle. And remember to hold on for dear life "HODL"

THE BITCOIN ADVOCATE
HAISAM SAID

INTRODUCTION

In an age of financial uncertainty, saving for the future has never been more critical. This book explores why Bitcoin, a decentralized digital currency, offers a unique opportunity for individuals to safeguard their wealth and prepare for unpredictable downtimes. In addition, you will learn how to invest in Bitcoin and understand chart patterns and candlestick terminology. This book will be a guide for you to refer to in your future of investing and trading!

THE ULTIMATE GUIDE FOR BEGINNERS!

ONE

Intro To Money

The barter system goes back 6000 years ago and has evolutionized with time through the 5 stages of money:

- Commodity money (i.e., grains, livestock)
- Metallic money (i.e., coins),
- Paper money (i.e., U.S. dollar, pound, peso)
- Credit in plastic form or currency of faith digital currency (i.e., PayPal, Bitcoin, crypto)

But let's fast forward….

Quick history lesson!!

Bretton woods system

The Bretton woods system required a currency to be tied to the dollar, which was also tied to the price of gold. The reason was to have everyone come to an agreement on a system of economic order and international cooperation that they believed would help countries recover from the devastation of war and would help long-term global growth!

What happened??

This system was in place until persistent united states-balance-of-payments deficits led to foreign-held dollars exceeding the United States gold stock, meaning that the United States could not complete its obligation to redeem dollars for gold at the official price.

In 1971 Richard Nixon ended the dollar's convertibility to gold!

America's debt and rapidly deteriorating payment situation made president Richard Nixon end the convertibility of the U.S. dollar to gold on August 15, 1971

So, what backs the U.S. dollar?

In the U.S., a single dollar was redeemable for gold until 1933. Over the last 100 years, governments have moved away from the gold standard. Currencies are now almost universally backed by governments that issue them. An example of a fiat currency is the dollar.

Today, the dollar is backed by two things: the government's ability to generate revenues via debt or taxes and its authority to compel economic participants to transact in dollars

Fiat money isn't good for several reasons!

Fiat money, like dollars, differs from commodity money such as gold or silver because it does not have intrinsic value. It's worth depends entirely on people's trust in the government that issues it. Central banks print unlimited amounts of fiat money, which can lead to inflation. When too much money circulates in the economy, its value can decrease quickly. The value of fiat currency is closely linked to the political and economic stability of the government that issues it. Political turmoil can lead to currency devaluation, a recent trend in several developing countries. Additionally, governments may misuse monetary policy through excessive money printing or poor fiscal management, destabilizing the currency. Over time, inflation can ruin the purchasing power of fiat money, making it less effective as a store of value.

WHAT CHANGED?

The U.S. dollar is no longer backed by gold due to a shift in monetary policy that began in the early 20th century and peaked in 1971 when President Nixon ended the dollar's convertibility into gold. This change was driven by several factors, including the increasing costs of maintaining gold reserves and the challenges posed by global economic pressures. Without the gold standard, the dollar now operates as a fiat currency. Its value is derived from trust in the government and the economy rather than a physical commodity. This system enables a more responsive monetary policy, allowing the Federal Reserve to adjust interest rates and manage inflation more effectively. As a result, it promotes economic stability and growth. The transition reflects a broader belief that a flexible currency can better meet the needs of a dynamic economy.

THE FEDERAL RESERVE!

The Federal Reserve act of 1913 gave authority to set monetary policy in the United States!

The Federal Reserve Banks are decentralized by design and are located in:

- Boston
- Philadelphia
- Atlanta
- Minneapolis
- New York
- Cleveland
- Chicago
- Kansas City
- New York
- Richmond
- St. Louis
- Dallas

- San Francisco

The Federal Reserve is a non-profit entity not owned by anyone but is managed by congress and the public!

By creating the Federal Reserve System, Congress intended to eliminate the severe financial crises that damaged the nation, especially the financial panic of 1907.

The Federal Reserve System is the central bank of the United States. It performs five essential functions to support the performance of the U.S. economy and serve the public interest.

The Federal Reserve:

1. Regulates the nation's monetary laws and policies to help promote high employment possibilities, stable prices, and attractive long-term interest rates in the economy.

2. Controls the stability of the financial system and aims to minimize and contain systemic risks through active monitoring and engagement both domestically and internationally.

3. Ensures the safety and soundness of individual financial institutions** and assesses their impact on the overall financial system.

4. Fosters the safety and efficiency of payments by providing services to the banks and the U.S. government that help facilitate U.S. dollar transactions and payments.

5. Gives consumer protection and community development through consumer-focused supervision and examination, community economic development activities, and enforcing consumer laws and regulations.

INFLATION!

What is inflation?

Inflation is the rate of increase in prices over a given period, such as the overall increase in prices or the increase in the cost of living!

What causes inflation?

If the supply falls but demand remains unchanged, upward pressure on prices and inflation occur. Therefore, inflation is pushed higher. For example, an increase in the price of domestic or imported goods (oils, raw materials) further increases the costs.

Who controls inflation?

As the federal reserve conducts monetary policy, it influences employment and inflation primarily by using its policy tools to affect overall financial conditions-including the availability and cost of credit in the economy.

How to stop inflation?

When confronting inflation, a government's central bank may take actions that reduce the nation's money supply. This is achieved through higher interest rates and changes in open market operations.

Who benefits from inflation?

Inflation allows borrowers to repay lenders with money that is worth less than when it was originally borrowed, which benefits borrowers. However, when inflation leads to higher prices, the demand for credit increases, resulting in higher interest rates, which benefits lenders.

NOTHING CHANGES IF NOTHING CHANGES!

TWO

INTRO TO BITCOIN!

WHAT IS BITCOIN?

It's a type of digital currency in which a record of transactions is maintained and the computational solution of mathematical problems generates new currency units, operating independently of a central bank!

Bitcoin is a decentralized digital payment system and currency. It was created by a person or group, going by the username Satoshi Nakamoto, who posted a whitepaper on a discussion board. Bitcoin operates without a financial system or government authorities and doesn't require the involvement of financial institutions.

Like all forms of currency, Bitcoin is given value by its users, supply, and demand. As long as it maintains the attributes associated with money and there is demand for it, it will remain a means of exchange, a store of value, and another way for investors to speculate regardless of its monetary value

As the asset's market value increases, Bitcoin makes money for investors through appreciation. A lot is going on behind the scenes in the Bitcoin network!

Bitcoin operates on a decentralized computer network, known as a distributed ledger, that tracks transactions in the cryptocurrency. When computers on this network verify and process transactions, new Bitcoins are made through a process called mining. These networked computers, referred to as miners, validate transactions in exchange for a payment in Bitcoin.

PLAN ₿ PLAYBOOK

Bitcoin mining is the process by which Bitcoin transactions are digitally validated on the network and added to the blockchain ledger. This involves solving complex cryptographic hash puzzles to confirm blocks of transactions that are updated on the decentralized blockchain.

As a decentralized system, Bitcoin functions without a central authority or a single administrator, allowing anyone to create a new Bitcoin address and conduct transactions without needing approval. This is made possible by the specialized distributed ledger known as the blockchain, which records all Bitcoin transactions.

Unlike traditional currencies, which central banks can print endlessly, Bitcoin introduces a groundbreaking concept: a limited supply. Capped at 21 million Bitcoins, scarcity is created, much like rare gems or precious metals. These historically have held value and appreciated over time.

21,000,000 Bitcoins, that's it! The race has started, and wealthy individuals and institutions are filling their bags with billions of dollars invested! It's just getting started, and you can still win!

BITCOIN TIMELINE

- Oct 31,2008 official white paper released- Satoshi Nakamoto published the Bitcoin whitepaper introducing the concept of a decentralized digital currency.

- Jan 3rd, 2009 genesis block mined- Bitcoin network officially launches with the mining of the first block.

- Oct 5th, 2009 first exchange rate- new liberty standard established Bitcoins at a first rate of 1,309BTC= $1 insane right!!!

- Nov 28th, 2012 first halving- block rewards reduce from 50BTC to 25BTC marking the first of Bitcoins planned Halvings.

- Dec 2013, Bitcoin hits $1,000 for the first time in history!

- July 2016, second halving- block rewards halve again from 25BTC to 12.5BTC

- Dec 2017, Bitcoin hits $20,000 creating a new high!

- May 2020 third halving- BTC block rewards are cut to 6.25BTC

- Oct 2021, first Bitcoin futures ETF launch, giving investors a new way to access Bitcoin

- Jan 2023, spot Bitcoin ETF approved, which became the most successful ETF in history!!!

- Mar 2024, fourth halving- block reward cut to 3.125BTC

BITCOIN PRICE TIMELINE!

- 2009 Bitcoin's inception - Price $0

- 2010 first record transaction - Price $0.0008-$0.08

- 2011 first price surge - Price $1-$31

- 2013 Bitcoin's breakthrough year - Price $13-$266

- 2014 Mt. Gox collapse - Price $500-$800

- 2017 Bitcoin hits an all-time high - Price $1000-$20,000

- 2018 bear market for Bitcoin - Price $6000- $13,000

- 2020-2021 institutional adoption and new ATH - Price $7,000-$64,000

- 2021-2022 recession fears market crash - Price $30,000-$69,000

- 2023 Bitcoin's recovery - Price $15,000-$30,000

- 2024 Bitcoins ongoing developments - Price $30,000

- Currently just broke through $81,000 and climbing as of November 2024

DECENTRALIZATION

Bitcoin's decentralized network is the foundation of its nature, distinguishing it from traditional currencies and financial systems. Bitcoin is a peer-to-peer network that operates without a central authority, such as a government or bank. Instead, it relies on a global network of computers that work together to validate and secure transactions all across the world.

The key components of the Bitcoin network are blockchain technology, mining and proof of work, computers and peer-to-peer communication, security and trust, and censorship resistance. Bitcoin operates on a global scale, so anyone with an internet connection can join in without needing any central authority. This allows for unbanked people or underbanked to access a global financial system. Bitcoins' decentralized network is the main reason for its success and attraction; it offers a transparent and secure alternative to traditional banking systems.

BITCOIN HALVINGS EVERY 4 YEARS!

Bitcoin Halvings are like the heartbeat of the cryptocurrency's system, pulsating in a rhythm set every four years to reduce the reward for mining new coins by half. Slowing supply growth reinforces Bitcoin scarcity and encourages a price increase as fewer new coins enter circulation. Halvings highlights the genius of the Bitcoin network's design, ensuring that the last Bitcoin won't be mined until 2140, more than 100 years from now, "2024," making it a long-term scarce asset.

The concept of hash rate, or the computation power used to secure the network and process transactions, plays a critical role in Bitcoin's value. The network becomes secure as the hash rate increases, making Bitcoin more trustworthy. This increased security underscores Bitcoin's appeal as a safe investment and a hedge against traditional financial system uncertainties like the 2008 housing crash that took down the economy and cost millions of families. Bitcoin is the best- performing asset of our time, and we are still early!

21,000,000 BITCOINS, LIMITED SUPPLY!

EACH BITCOIN WILL BE WORTH MILLIONS ONE DAY!

SAVING IN BITCOIN!

Saving in Bitcoin has never been easier with the accessibility and rise of digital wallets and easy-to-use platforms.

WHY SAVE IN BITCOIN?

- Bitcoin has historically shown significant price appreciation over an extended period, offering the potential for high returns compared to traditional savings.

- With a cap of a supply of 21 million coins, bitcoin is a hedge against inflation, protecting purchasing power as fiat currencies may depreciate.

- Bitcoin operates on a decentralized network, not relying on banks and governments, which can be to the liking of those who seek financial independence.

- Bitcoin can be available and used by anyone with an internet connection, also providing financial services to those without access to traditional banks.

- More businesses and institutions are adopting bitcoin, increasing its legitimacy and usability as a form of payment and store of value.

- Bitcoin transactions are secured by cryptography and the blockchain, making it difficult to counterfeit or double-spend.

- Including Bitcoin in your investment portfolio can provide diversification, potentially reducing overall risk.

- Bitcoin allows users to have full control of their assets, which enhances privacy and security.

- Bitcoin is one of the most liquid assets available, allowing for quick and easy buying and selling on tons of exchanges.

- Overall, many believe Bitcoin could play a central role in the future of finance and possibly become the global reserve asset!

> "Bitcoin is an international asset;
> it's not based on anyone's currency"!
> – Larry Fink
> Black Rock CEO

HODL!

SAVE IN BITCOIN & GROW WITH BITCOIN!

START SMALL! OR START BIG!
JUST START!

SATOSHIS

Satoshis are the smallest unit of Bitcoin, named after its anonymous creator Satoshi Nakamoto. Here's how the breakdown goes in Bitcoin terms:

- One Bitcoin is divisible into 100 million Satoshis. This means 1 Satoshi is equal to 0.00000001 BTC.

- Satoshis enable micro-transactions, making it easy to send very small amounts of Bitcoin, which is crucial for applications like tipping or small payments.

- The ability to use Satoshis allows for precise transactions and flexibility in pricing, catering to all types of user needs.

- By allowing investments in smaller increments, Satoshis make Bitcoin more accessible to a broader audience, allowing people to invest in Bitcoin without needing to buy the whole coin itself.

- As Bitcoin price increases, the value of a single Satoshi grows, emphasizing Bitcoin potential as a store of value!

You have the opportunity of a lifetime to save and stack sats now!

STACK SATS!!!!

SATOSHI BREAKDOWN!

1 Satoshi = 0.00000001
10 Satoshi = 0.00000010
100 Satoshi= 0.00000100
1000 Satoshi= 0.00001000
10,000 Satoshi= 0.00010000
100,000 Satoshi= 0.00100000
1,000,000 Satoshi= 0.01000000
10,000,000 Satoshi= 0.10000000
100,000,000 Satoshi= 1.00000000

You don't have to buy 1 Bitcoin; a Satoshi is the smallest unit of Bitcoin!

The growth of a $10,000 investment 10 years ago in these different investments would be

- NVidia stock - $714,000

- Bitcoin- 1,500,000

- Microsoft- $100,000

- Gold- 16,000

- Savings account- $10,500

Investing is mandatory with how inflation is running and history always repeats itself!

BREAKING DOWN SATOSHIS IN DOLLARS!

1 BITCOIN = 100,000,000 SATS
1 SAT = 0.00000001 BTC

For example:

1 BITCOIN = $30,000
1 SAT = 0.0003

The value of Satoshis in dollars fluctuates based on the current market price of Bitcoin. The formula is to calculate the current price of Bitcoin and divide it by 100,000,000.

The value of a Satoshi is susceptible to Bitcoin's market price. For example:

- If Bitcoin's price rises from $30,000 to $60,000, the value of a Satoshi doubles from $0.0003 to $0.0005.

- Conversely, if Bitcoin drops from $30,000 to $15,000, the value of a Satoshi decreases from $0.0003 to $0.00015.

This price fluctuation makes the value of Satoshis dynamic, requiring ongoing calculations to assess how much a Satoshi is worth in real-time.

DCA

Dollar-cost averaging (DCA) is an investment strategy where an investor consistently invests a fixed amount of money at regular intervals, regardless of market conditions. This approach helps mitigate the risk of making significant investments at inopportune times, such as during market highs. By spreading out investments, DCA allows the investor to purchase more shares when prices are low and fewer when prices are high, potentially lowering the average cost per share over time. This strategy can be particularly beneficial for long-term investors, as it encourages disciplined investing, reduces emotional decision-making, and takes advantage of market volatility. While it doesn't eliminate the risks of investing, dollar cost averaging can help smooth out the impact of market fluctuations, especially for those not actively managing their portfolios daily.

BITCOINS FUTURE

Bitcoin, the world's first cryptocurrency, has come a long way since its creation, but it's still early. As a digital asset and decentralized financial system, Bitcoin has sparked global interest and revolutionized the way people think about money, transactions, and value storage. As we look into the future of Bitcoin, several key factors will influence its evolution: adoption and role in the global economy. It will depend on the ability to scale, adapt to regulatory demands, maintain its decentralization, and address environmental concerns. While the future is not entirely clear, the Bitcoin future is very bright and will remain a central figure in the digital economy and become the world's greatest store of value in the future. One of the most significant aspects of Bitcoin's future is its continued adoption by both individuals and institutions. Over the past few years, more companies, financial institutions, and even countries have started integrating Bitcoin into their operations. Institutions like MicroStrategy, tesla, and square have invested billions in Bitcoin, seeing it as a store of value and a hedge against inflation. The potential for Bitcoin to be adopted as legal tender is similar to El Salvador's experiment. It can set a precedent for other nations to follow, especially in countries with unstable currencies.

BITCOIN WILL BE THE BIGGEST AND GREATEST TRANSFER OF WEALTH!

EL SALVADOR & BITCOIN

In September 2021, the country El Salvador made history by becoming the first country in the world to adopt Bitcoin as a legal tender, a move aimed at promoting financial inclusion and boosting the economy. President Nayib Bukele advocated for the integration of Bitcoin to facilitate remittances,

Attract foreign investments and reduce reliance on traditional financial systems. The law mandated that Bitcoin be accepted for all transactions, allowing citizens use it alongside the U.S. dollar which had been the country's official currency since 2001. To support the initiative, and the government launched a digital wallet called "Chivo" offering incentives like Bitcoin bonuses for its users. Despite facing skepticism and challenges including volatility and infrastructural issues. El Salvador's bold experiment sparked global discussions about cryptocurrency adoption and the future of money. This showed both the potential benefits and risks of integrating digital currencies into national economies. El Salvador buys 1 Bitcoin daily!

BITCOIN & INSTITUTIONS

In the coming years, Bitcoin could see further integration into traditional financial markets, with more financial products based on Bitcoin, such as ETFs, futures, and options, being launched. If Bitcoin becomes more embedded in the global economic system, it could further legitimize its status as an asset class and encourage even more excellent institutional investment.

Governments and central banks are also exploring more options in digital currencies, such as Central Bank Digital Currencies (CBDCS), to help modernize their financial systems.

While CBDC would likely operate differently from Bitcoin, it could influence how governments view cryptocurrencies. The rise of CBDCS could complement or challenge Bitcoin, depending on how they are designed and implemented.

ONLY 0.27% OF GLOBAL POPULATION CAN OWN 1 BITCOIN EACH

BITCOIN FUN FACTS

- Bitcoin is the first and oldest crypto coin
- The maximum number of Bitcoins is 21 million, but the last Bitcoin won't be mined for 100 years

- Bitcoins network has been functional without error for over 13 years with a 99.99% rate

- Satoshi Nakamoto, the creator of Bitcoin, vanished after creating Bitcoin. His, or their, identity is unknown

- The first recorded Bitcoin transaction was 10,000BTC for two pizzas from Papa John's worth $25, so now May 22nd is Bitcoin pizza day

- Bitcoins blockchain is beamed to the whole world via satellite

What makes Bitcoin so unique is the blockchain technology is immutable, which means no entity can erase or alter any information on the network. One of the greatest public ledger to ever be created.

TYPES OF STORAGES

- **Hot Wallets:** online wallets for quick access, for example, mobile or web wallets

- **Cold Wallets:** offline wallets for quick access, for example (hardware wallets) for enhanced security

- **Reputable exchanges** such as Coinbase, Binance, kraken, Robinwood, the list goes on...

On popular exchanges, you will need to create an account by signing up for the exchange of your choice, verifying your identity, and linking your bank account or payment method. At this point, you are all set to make your first purchase, deciding how much Bitcoin you want to buy. Start small if you're new. You can purchase fractions of a Bitcoin thanks to Satoshis. After purchasing your Bitcoin or sats, you have the option of leaving it on the exchange or transferring it to your wallet of choice for more added security and long- term holding!

BITCOIN STRATEGIC NATIONAL RESERVE!

A Bitcoin Strategic National Reserve (BSNR) is a proposed concept where a nation or government accumulates and holds Bitcoin as a strategic asset, much like traditional reserves such as gold or foreign currency. The idea behind a BSNR is to utilize Bitcoin's decentralized, borderless, and deflationary characteristics to hedge against economic instability, currency devaluation, and geopolitical risks. As Bitcoin continues to grow in prominence as a store of value, nations may choose to build reserves to bolster their financial security, enhance global influence, and diversify their reserves away from traditional fiat currencies.

The strategic reserve could serve multiple functions, such as:

- **Hedge against inflation:** Bitcoin's limited supply (21 million coins) makes it resistant to inflationary pressures that affect fiat currencies. With the rise of digital currencies and world trade tensions, Bitcoin offers an alternative to foreign currency reserves. It is an asset that is not subject to the control of any single central bank or government.

- **Financial sovereignty:** By holding Bitcoin, a nation could reduce its dependence on international financial institutions and avoid potential sanctions or economic manipulation.

- **National security:** In times of crisis or war, Bitcoin's decentralized nature provides an asset that is difficult to seize or block by foreign powers.

Implementing a Bitcoin Strategic National Reserve would require careful management, including balancing Bitcoin's volatility with the stability needs of the national economy. Governments would need to establish frameworks for buying, securing, and possibly using Bitcoin in a way that aligns with broader economic goals and geopolitical strategies. Some countries, like El Salvador, have already begun integrating Bitcoin into their economies, though the idea of a national reserve is still in its early conceptual stages.

BITCOIN VS EVERYONE!

Bitcoin has evolved to where now you can send money anywhere in the world instantly via the internet, not needing to go to the bank or struggle with western union. Bitcoin offers several advantages over western union for transferring money. First, it provides faster transaction times, often completing transfers within minutes compared to western union, which can take hours or even days depending on the method used. Even locating a western union can be difficult, depending on where you are. Bitcoin eliminates all of this!!! Bitcoin transactions can be more cost- effective, especially for international transfers, as they often involve lower fees than traditional services that charge a percentage or a fixed fee. Bitcoin operates on a decentralized network, which means it is not subject to the same regulatory restrictions as the western union. This can enhance privacy and security for users. Bitcoin is accessible to anyone with an internet connection. Bitcoin allows users to retain control of their funds without relying on a third party. Overall, Bitcoin represents a modern alternative to money transfers, making it accessible globally to anyone via the internet, offering instant transfers, low costs, and greater autonomy.

Bitcoin is the greatest asset of our time and quickest growing!

Think of it as a store of value/asset that is easily convertible to fiat if needed. Compared to real estate, you can't walk around with a house or apartment, and it would take some time if you wanted to sell and get the cash for it. The same goes for gold; nobody is walking around with tons of kilos of gold in their pocket, this is what separates Bitcoin!

BITCOIN'S MARKET CAP IS AT $1.8 TRILLION AS OF NOV 2024.

THERE'S OVER $800 TRILLION IN ASSETS IN THE WORLD.

GOLD MARKET CAP IS AT $17 TRILLION AS OF NOV 2024.

BITCOIN WILL BE WORTH $600K EACH WHEN IT GETS TO GOLDS MARKET CAP.

THREE

HOW TO START INVESTING?

WAYS TO INVEST IN BITCOIN

- **Direct purchase:** buy Bitcoin directly from an exchange and hold it in your wallet or exchange

- **Dollar Cost Avg (DCA):** invest a fixed amount of money at regular intervals (e.g., weekly or monthly) to mitigate market volatility. This is a very popular method with proven positive statistics.

- **Bitcoin ETFs:** consider investing in exchange-traded funds (ETFs) that track Bitcoin price, offering exposure without needing to hold Bitcoin directly.

- **Bitcoin mining:** invest in mining equipment to earn Bitcoin by validating transactions. But this requires more technical knowledge and a significant investment

- **Peer-to-peer trading:** use platforms that facilitate direct trades between users, allowing more flexible pricing and payment options

- **Bitcoin savings accounts:** some platforms offer interest on Bitcoin deposits, allowing you to earn passive income

- **Bitcoin futures and options:** trade derivatives that allow you to get in on Bitcoin price movements without owning the asset directly. This approach requires knowledge of trading that we will be explain later in the book

- **Always stay informed and keep up with the news and market trends;** remember to use risk management by investing only what you can afford to lose, and always remember to diversify!

WHY SHOULD I INVEST?

Investing in Bitcoin can offer potential benefits compared to saving in FIAT.

- Bitcoin has proved that it has recorded higher returns than most assets compared to traditional savings accounts, which offer low interest to you.

- Bitcoin can help preserve purchasing power; fiat currencies lose value due to inflations. Lately, it's been on a steep decline while assets like Bitcoin have been appreciating against it.

- Investing in Bitcoin helps you diversify your portfolio, reducing the risk of just holding cash.

As volatile as Bitcoin is, it can offer huge growth opportunities as we are still early to it.

Bitcoin is a long-term play. Look at it as a savings account instead of investing. You don't touch it and keep putting money in it. Your account will grow; the more sats you stack, the closer you get to a full coin. Dollar cost average is the best way to do it, whether weekly or monthly, whatever works for you. As long as you stick to your plan, purchasing ($10, $20, $100, $1000) weekly or monthly and don't touch your account, it will grow. Be sure to invest at your own risk first; only invest what you can afford to lose. Also, know to watch the market conditions and the news because things change and the market gets affected by it. Be cautious when trading and investing.

ACCOUNT SETUP MOST ACCOUNTS

Creating a Coinbase or an exchange of your choice, there are many to choose from, is an easy process:

- Visit the Coinbase website or download the app, click on "get started" and fill in your personal information, including your name, email, and password. You'll receive a confirmation email to verify your address.

- After confirming your email, log in and complete the identity verification; this involves uploading a government-issued id and possibly a photo to comply with standard regulations.

- Enable two-factor authentication (2FA) for added security; this involves linking your phone number for SMS or using an authenticator app like google authenticator.

- Once all that is completed, you can add a payment method to buy Bitcoin. You have multiple ways of doing this. You can link a bank account, Coinbase gift card, debit card or credit card, and bank transfers, but those tend to take longer.

- Once your account is set up and funded, go to the "buy/sell" tab, select Bitcoin, and enter the amount you want to purchase after reviewing the transaction details and confirming your order.

- After purchasing, your Bitcoin will appear in your Coinbase wallet. If you want added security, you can consider transferring it to a personal wallet with your keys.

That's it, all done!

FOUR

INTRO TO TRADING

Trading is an act of buying and selling financial instruments like stocks, forex, or cryptocurrencies like Bitcoin to make a profit. It's essential to understand fundamental concepts like market orders, limit orders, and how different markets operate before diving into it. Many people are drawn to trading by the freedom and potential profit you can make from it but also fail to realize that trading is not a get rich overnight idea it requires strategy, discipline, and constant learning. In trading, understanding the balance between risk and reward is vital because successful traders evaluate potential risks carefully and develop strategies to manage them while aiming for favorable returns on their investments. Trading can be approached in many ways, such as day trading, swing trading, or long-term investing. Each style has its own risk profile, time commitment, and strategies, making it essential find one that goes with your goals and personality.

Effective trading often relies on two main types of analysis: fundamental and technical. Fundamental analysis involves evaluating a company's financial health, while technical analysis focuses on price patterns and market trends. Both methods can help inform your trading decisions.

Successful trading involves both psychology and strategy. Controlling emotions like fear and greed is important for making rational decisions and sticking to your trading plan, especially in volatile markets. Before you start trading, it's essential to define your goals. Are you looking to generate supplemental income, save for a specific objective, or build long-term wealth? Setting clear expectations for yourself will guide your trading strategy and risk management, which we will discuss later.

TRADING VS. INVESTING

Trading and investing are two different ways of participating in financial markets, each with different goals, strategies, and time horizons. Trading typically involves short-term buying and selling of assets, with positions often held for just seconds, minutes, or days. Traders usually seek to capitalize on market fluctuations and price movements. Investing focuses on long-term growth. Investors buy assets with the mindset to hold them for years or even decades, aiming to benefit from the underlying value appreciation and dividends. Traders usually aim to generate quick profits from market volatility. Their strategy revolves around timing the market and taking advantage of price discrepancies, while investors seek to build wealth gradually through the appreciation of their investments over time.

Their focus is on the fundamental value of assets instead of the short-term price movements. Trading relies heavily on technical analysis, using charts, indicators, and patterns to inform decisions. Traders often use strategies like day trading, swing trading, and scalping. As for investing, it typically involves fundamental analysis, assessing a company's financial health or history of crypto coin, growth potential and overall economic conditions. Investors prioritize long-term metrics such as earnings, cash flow, and market position. Traders generally accept higher levels of risk as they do more transactions and are exposed more to market volatility compared to investors who often adopt a more conservative approach focusing on stability and long-term performance. Traders must maintain strict discipline, often making quick decisions based on market conditions as investors usually have a long-term perspective, which helps against emotional reactions. Tunnel vision on the end goal.

FIVE

RISK MANAGEMENT & LEVERAGE

Risk management and leveraging involve a lot of knowledge and strategy:

- **Position sizing:** determine the size of each trade based on your total capital and risk tolerance. A common rule is to risk no more than 1-2% of your trading capital on a single trade, making sure that no single loss can impact your overall portfolio.

- **Stop-loss orders:** get used to using a stop-loss because that will save your trade and mind. Implementing stop-loss orders automatically closes a trade at a set price, limiting the potential loss. This helps protect your capital.

- **Take-profit orders:** this allows you to lock in profits by closing a position once it reaches a price you set.

Leverage allows traders to control larger positions than their capital would normally allow, but it also increases risk. Use leverage conservatively. Establish a risk-to-reward ratio before entering a trade. For example, aim for a ratio of 1:2, meaning you expect to gain twice as much as you risk. This approach helps ensure that even a lower win rate, you can still be profitable. Adjust your trading strategy based on market volatility and conditions. In highly volatile markets, consider reducing your position sizes or avoid leverage to control risk. Be aware of the psychological aspects of trading, such as fear and greed. Having a clear risk management plan helps you stay disciplined and prevent emotional decisions.

In the next coming pages, you will learn about the common candlestick and chart patterns. I will break them down on how to identify them and what each of them means. This is to be used as a reference for yourself in your future trading journey that you can study or refer back to.

SIX

CANDLESTICK AND CHART PATTERNS!

THIS IS FOR ANYONE WANTING TO LEARN CHARTS AND HOW TO TRADE!!!

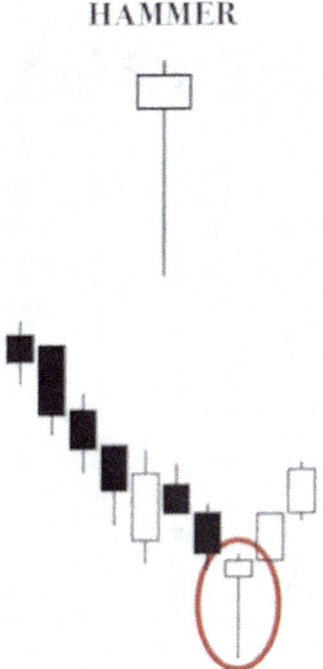

The hammer is a bullish sign that appears during a downtrend. It has a small body located close to the top of the trading range and a lengthy lower shadow. This structure indicates that bears pushed prices down during the session, but bulls regained control by the session's close. The hammer pattern suggests that bullish momentum may be building, making it an important indicator for traders to watch for a potential price increase. Traders typically view this signal as a buy or long opportunity.

HANGING MAN

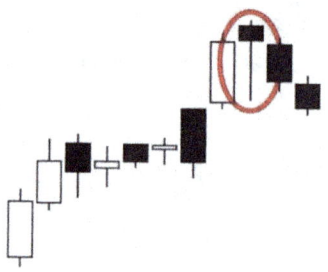

The hanging man is a candlestick pattern that shows at the end of an uptrend and signals a potential reversal to a downtrend. It has a small body near the top of the trading range with a long lower shadow, indicating that bears tried to push the prices down, but bulls managed to bring them back up by the close. This pattern lets traders know that bull pressure may be weakening and lets traders consider selling or shorting.

<u>INVERTED HAMMER</u>

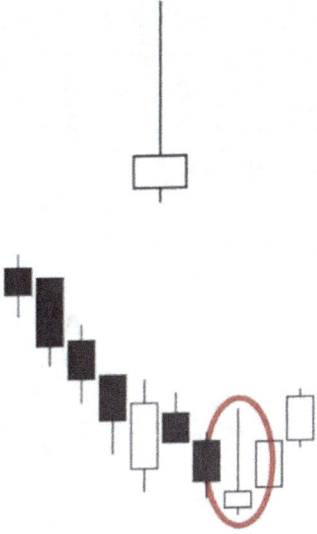

The inverted hammer is a bullish reversal sign that forms during a downtrend. It gets its name because it signifies that the market is "hammering out" a bottom. This pattern occurs when the price has declined and suggests a reversal potential. The long upper shadow indicates that buyers attempted to push the price higher. Traders typically interpret this signal as a buy or long signal, especially when subsequent bullish candles confirm it.

SHOOTING STAR

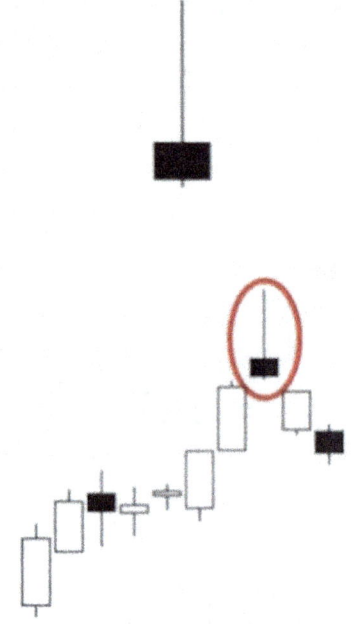

The shooting star is a bearish reversal sign indicating a market top or a strong resistance level. This pattern resembles the inverted hammer but occurs after a price increase. Traders view it as a sell or short signal, mainly when it follows a strong uptrend.

BEARISH ENGULFING

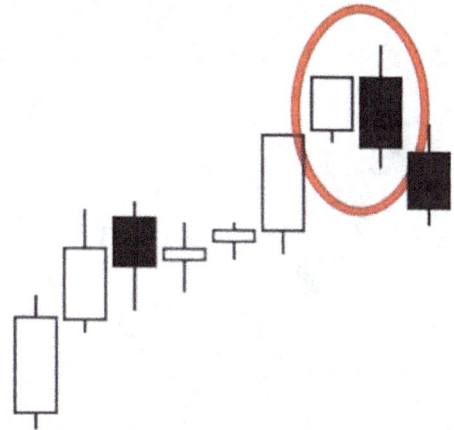

The bearish engulfing pattern is a candlestick formation that signals a potential reversal from bullish to bearish. It happens when a smaller, bullish candle is followed by a larger, bearish candle that engulfs the previous one. This pattern lets traders know that the sellers have gained control and could start sending prices down. This signal is good to consider shorting the asset or selling.

BULLISH ENGULFING

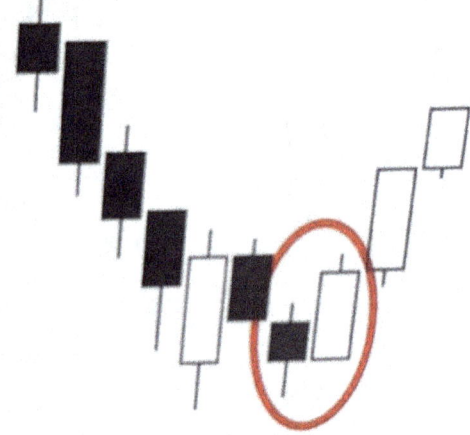

The bullish engulfing pattern is a two-candlestick a reversal pattern that signals that a strong up move could occur, and it happens when a bearish candle is immediately followed by a larger bullish candle. Traders see this as a strong buy signal, especially when it appears at support levels or after a downtrend.

TWEEZER BOTTOM

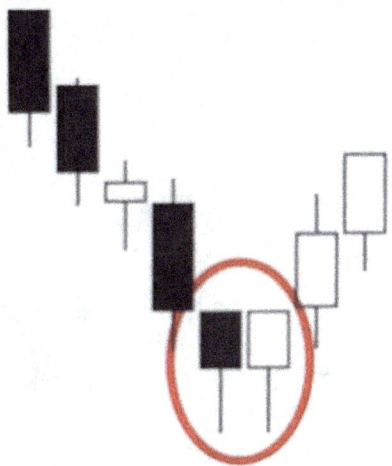

Tweezer bottoms are a bullish reversal pattern that forms at the end of a downtrend. This pattern lets traders know that bears are losing momentum and bulls are gaining traction. Traders see this as a signal to buy or go long.

TWEEZER TOPS

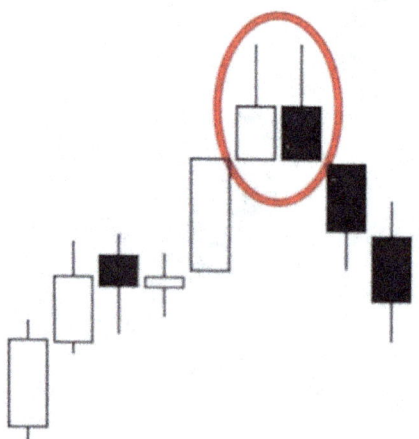

The tweezer tops is a bearish reversal pattern that occurs at the end of an uptrend. This pattern lets traders know that bulls are losing momentum and sellers are gaining traction. Traders see this as a sell or short signal.

MORNING STAR

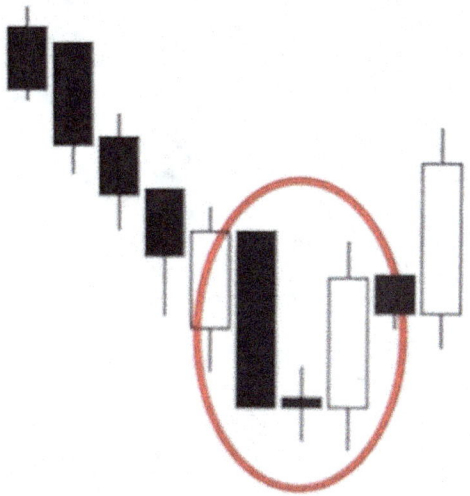

Morning star is a triple candlestick bullish reversal sign that typically occurs at the bottom of a downtrend. A large bearish candle, followed by a smaller indecisive candle (which can be bullish or bearish), and then a large bullish candle. The morning star indicates that bears are slowing down and bulls are gaining momentum. Traders view this pattern as a strong signal to buy or enter long positions.

EVENING STAR

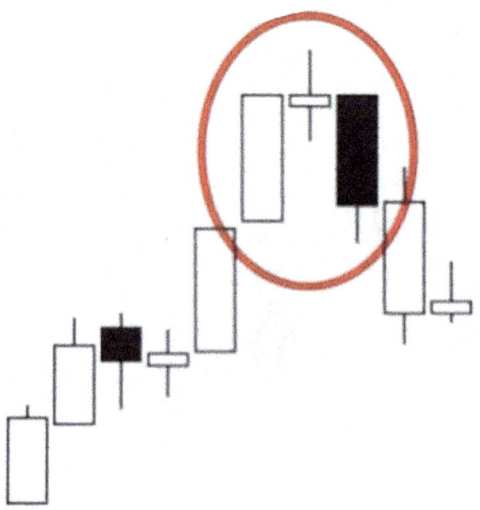

Evening star is a triple candlestick pattern opposite to the morning star. It is a bearish reversal that usually forms at the top of an uptrend. It has a large bullish candle, followed by a smaller indecisive candle that can be (bullish or bearish) and a large bearish candle. This pattern lets traders know that bulls are losing momentum and bears are starting to catch traction. This is usually considered a strong signal to sell or short.

THREE WHITE SOLDIERS

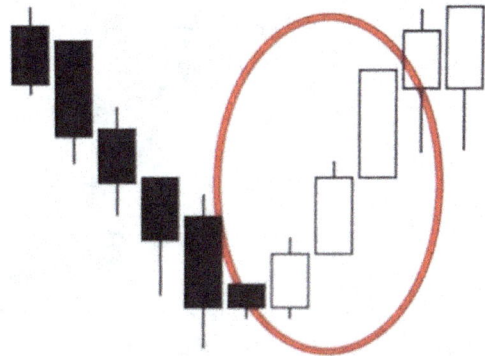

The first candle in the "Three White Soldiers" pattern is the Reversal Candle. This candle indicates either the end of a downtrend or suggests that a period of consolidation following the downtrend has concluded.

For this pattern to be considered valid, the second candlestick must be larger than the first. The second and third candlesticks should also close near their highs, leaving only a tiny wick. Traders interpret this signal as a strong buy, anticipating further upward movement.

THREE BLACK CROWS

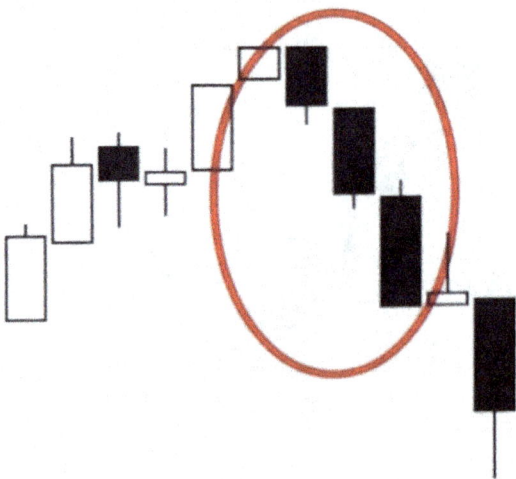

Three black crows, the first candlestick is called the reversal candle. It either ends the uptrend or implies that the time of consolidation that went after the uptrend is over. To be valid, the second candlestick should be bigger than the previous candles body. The second candlestick should close near its high, leaving a small wick, and the same for the third candlestick. Traders usually see this signal a sell or short.

THREE INSIDE UP

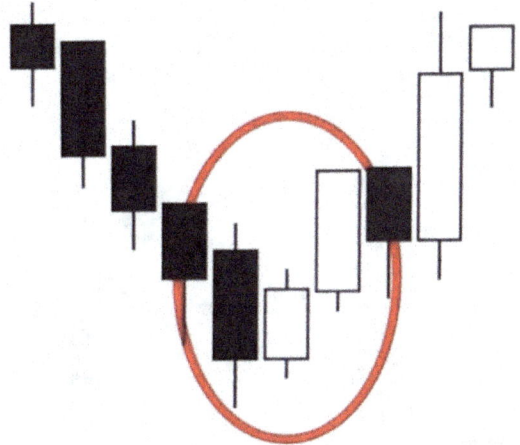

Three inside up candlestick formation is a trend reversal pattern found at a down trend's bottom. The triple candlestick pattern indicates the downtrend is possibly over, and the new uptrend has started. Traders see this signal as a buy or long.

THREE INSIDE DOWN

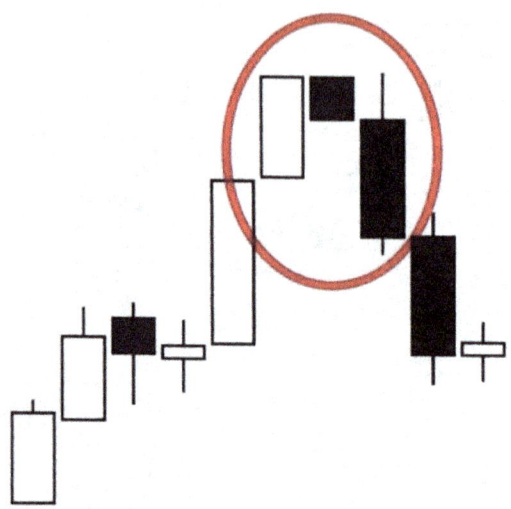

Three inside down candlestick formation is a trend reversal pattern found at an uptrend top. This pattern also indicates the uptrend is possibly over, and the new downtrend has started. Traders use this signal as a sell or short.

ASCENDING TRIANGLE

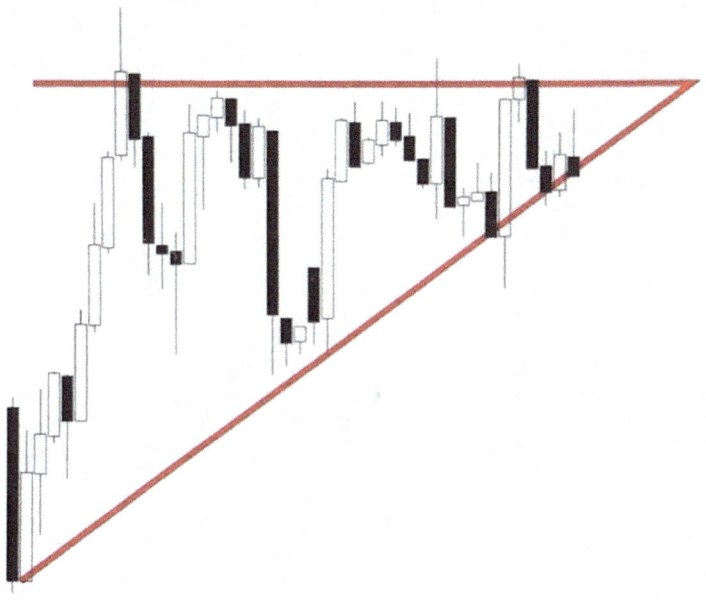

Ascending triangle is a chart pattern that happens when there is a resistance level and a slope of higher lows. This can go either way, but most of the time, it's bullish, and the price rises. Traders see this as a potential buy signal.

DESCENDING TRIANGLE

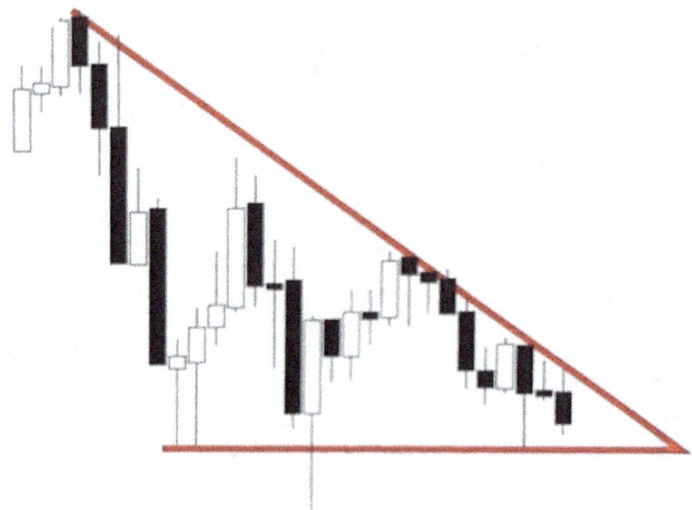

The descending triangle is the trend of lower highs that form the upper line. The lower line is a support level that the price cannot break. The example shows the price making lower highs, meaning there is more selling pressure. Traders see this signal as a sell or short.

RISING WEDGE

A rising wedge is a bearish reversal sign that forms during an uptrend. This pattern indicates that while the prices are going higher, the rate of increase is slowing, meaning bulls are tired. Traders consider this as a signal to sell or short.

SYMMETRICAL TRIANGLE

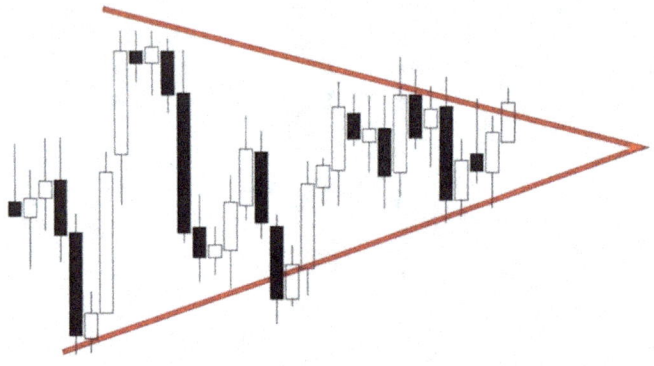

A symmetrical triangle is a continuation pattern. This sign indicates a period of consolidation and uncertainty in the market as bulls and bears are in balance. The breakout direction can be upward or downward, and it typically occurs after the price has been contained within the triangle for some time. Traders often look for confirmation of the breakout with increased volume, using it as a signal to enter a position in the breakout. Traders often look for increased volume to confirm the breakout direction, using it as a signal to enter a position.

FALLING WEDGE

Falling wedge is a bullish reversal sign that typically forms during a downtrend. This pattern indicates that while prices are still falling, the rate of decline is slowing. This means bears are slowing down. A breakout above the upper trend signals a shift in momentum, usually leading to a reversal and uptrend in price. Traders use this as a buy signal.

DOUBLE TOP

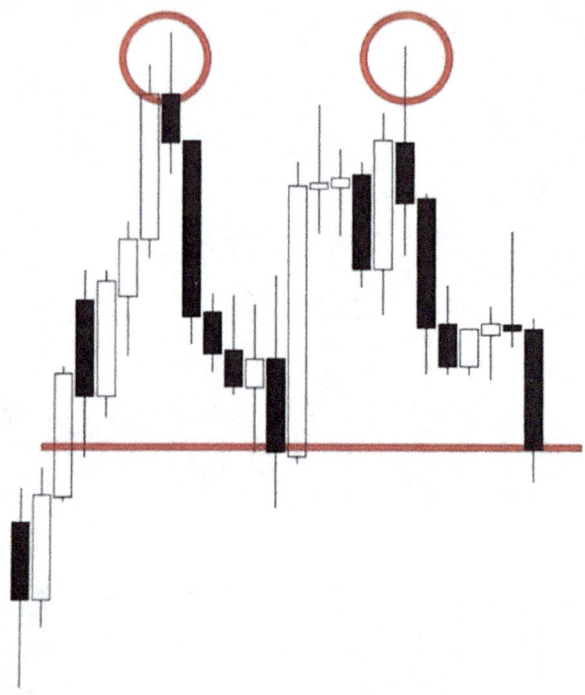

Double top is a reversal pattern formed after a wide move up. The two peaks at the top are a strong sign that a reversal is on its way, and the buying pressure died down. Traders see this signal to sell or short.

DOUBLE BOTTOM

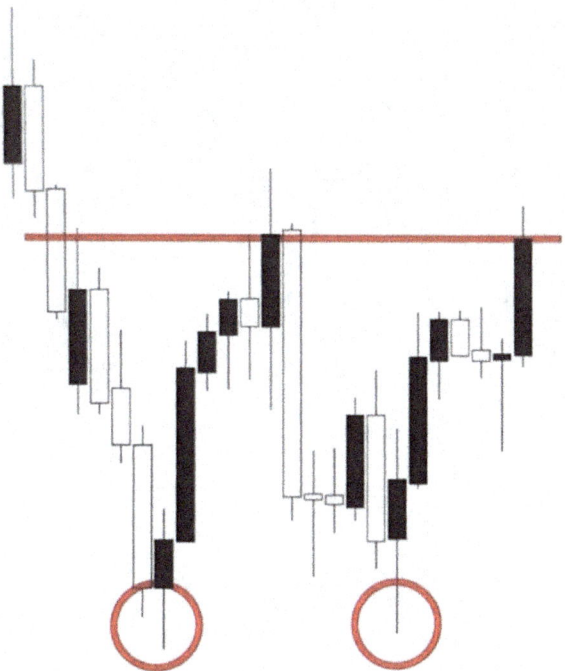

Double bottom pattern is a trend reversal formation. This is a time to go long bullish instead of short. This occurs after continued downtrends when two bottoms have formed. Also showing a reversal is about to happen because the selling pressure died down. Traders see this signal as a buy or to go long.

HEAD AND SHOULDERS

The head and shoulders sign is a trend reversal formation. It's formed by a shoulder followed by a higher head and a lower shoulder. As you can see, the head is the second and highest point with the two shoulders on each side. This tends to lead to a bearish pattern. Traders see this pattern as a signal to sell or short.

INVERSE HEAD AND SHOULDERS

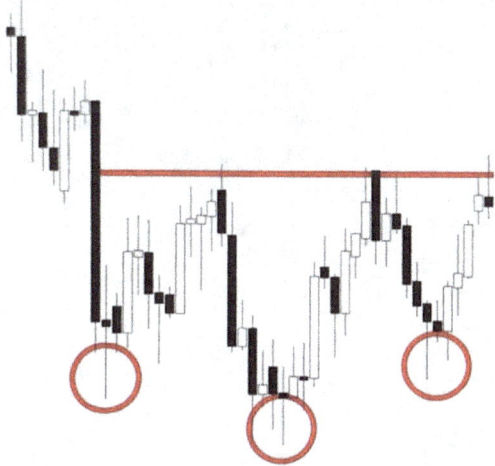

Inverse head and shoulders pattern is also a trend reversal formation. It's pretty much a head and shoulders formation but upside down. A shoulder is formed followed by a lower head and a higher shoulder. These usually occur after continued downward movements. Traders see this as a bullish reversal signal to buy or go long.

BULLISH PENNANT

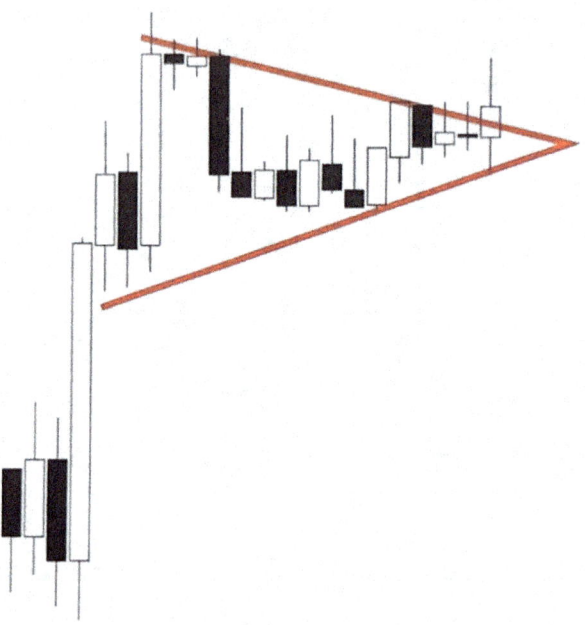

Bullish pennants are signals that the bulls are about to take over again; the climb up on price would continue after that area of consolidation until the bulls gather enough momentum to take the price higher again. Traders see this as a buy signal for more gains to come.

BEARISH PENNANT

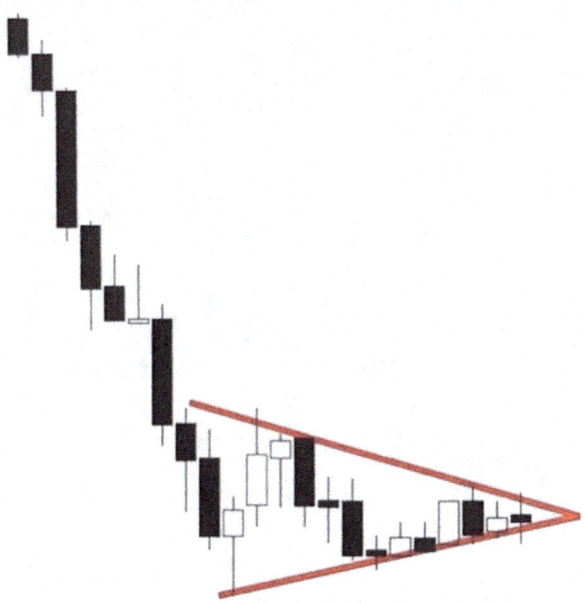

Bearish pennant occurs during a steep kind of vertical downtrend. After that there's a sharp price drop. Some sellers usually close their positions while other sellers decide to join in, making the price consolidate for a bit more. As soon as enough sellers jump in, the price breaks below the bottom of the pennant and continues to go down further. Traders see this as a sell signal or short.

BULLISH RECTANGLE

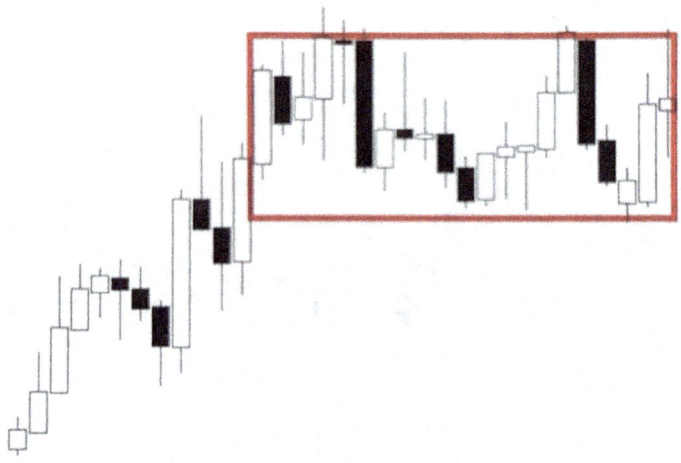

The bullish rectangle is after an uptrend. The price starts to consolidate, a sign that the price is going to move higher. Traders see this signal as a buy signal or long.

BEARISH RECTANGLE

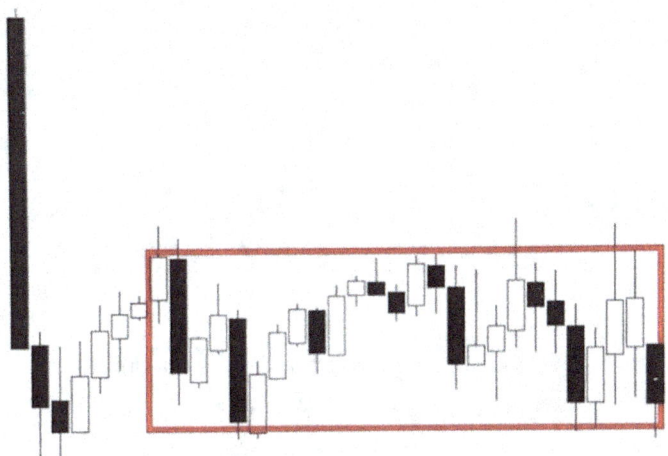

A bearish rectangle is a continuation pattern that occurs during an uptrend and signals a potential price reversal. The price moves sideways within the range, creating a rectangular shape, as shown above. This pattern forms when bulls and bears are in a temporary equilibrium. A breakout below the support level indicates sellers ' gained control, often leading to further downtrend movement. This pattern is a signal to sell or short.

BITCOIN IS WORTH WHAT PEOPLE ARE WILLING TO PAY FOR IT!

I might not change the world, but I guarantee you
I'll spark the brain of the one who will!

— Tupac Shakur

Endnote

I wrote this book to help anyone that wants to better themselves and their future. This book is a playbook that can introduce you into the world of finance economics, trading, and future of money.

Bitcoin!

I hope you will find it helpful with all the information provided to you so you can begin your journey into investing and saving for your future. Times are changing and if you're not adapting and growing and changing with it you will be left behind. Use this book as a guide into your future of managing your finances and bettering your lifestyle. And remember to H.O.D.L

THE BITCOIN ADVOCATE
HAISAM SAID

@THEBITCOINADVOCATE

ISBN: 979834590079

NOTES

www.ingramcontent.com/pod-product-compliance
Lightning Source LLC
Chambersburg PA
CBHW052337220526
45472CB00001B/459